MUSINGS OF A HUMAN BEING

BOOK TWO

BARRY H. MANSFIELD

Trafford
PUBLISHING®   www.trafford.com
North America & international
toll-free: 1 888 232 4444 (USA & Canada)
fax: 812 355 4082

CONTENTS

My name is Barry H Mansfield, I consider myself to be a philosophical poet. I have been published in several journals. One that comes to mind is a "journal for ordinary though' 2007 where my poem **"The way I think"**, was first published. Also, in Northeastern's independent. My first book **"Thrown out of the Garden"** will be published this year. My poems are about the possibility of creating something good out of something that's not so much. I have been going to school for a very long time, trying to increase my understanding of the world in which we live so that I can help create, if I'm allowed to a possible better future for as many as I can.

It is my belief, to understand one's path into the future it is necessary to know the history behind the quest. In this case I think that I should start by saying I've always had an extreme dyslexic-dysgraphic problem. It is a problem which caused me great consternation in my formative education. Still it did not stop me from gaining my GED while I was in the Army. It did not stop me from becoming one of my units' best helicopter mechanics. But it did limit me in the occupations I could pursue after my enlistment was over. I wanted more, I wanted to feel like I was accomplishing something or at least being productive.

So, I came up with a plan, the physical act of writing was extremely difficult, any kind of prose was almost beyond my ability. The thought was, that if I could write simple poems, thereby practicing my writing skills that I could one day write more comprehensive and detailed prose.

The first step of my plan was to find poems that I liked and understood and to say the same thing that the poem said by changing every word in the poem I had chosen. After practicing this exercise multiple times and finding that I could do this well, I decided it was time to throw away the practice and create something of my own. The first poem that I wrote had to be something that was on my mind and of use in my future endeavors. It goes like this.

What magic in the darkness among the treasures in our minds?
what fortunes and what blessings can we find
of the power and enlightenment that here too in do dwell
can we find our true fulfillment, and escape this earthbound hell

To me this poem had a lot of meaning and part of that meeting was to unlock my hidden abilities, I had first to gain knowledge. At that point the gaining of knowledge became more than something that was fun it became something that to me was necessary.

My formative Education, except for the time that I went to school in Lake Bluff and Lake Forest was a true disaster. Knowing that, I could not let the past hold me Back from what I needed to do. I started this process by enrolling at Truman College. When I enroll their, the counselors that I spoke to were not very helpful in helping me to form a plan which would lead me towards graduation. Undaunted I proceeded to make this experience my own. So, I chose to take classes in which I felt I could excel. I join student government, drama club, video club, and took part in creating a new theater group. I did extremely well in 98% of the classes that I took achieving in my time there a 3.25 grade average and earning myself 97 credit hours. I was proud of myself

Many of the courses that I took at this time alleviated my ignorance and allowed me to understand much more than I previously had It also formed the springboard of my creativity, allowing me to write many of the poems that went into the first book I had published. Which is entitled "Thrown out of the Garden" by Barry H Mansfield.

Unfortunately, before this happened my father died and being the sensitive individual that I am I became somewhat depressed. And that and the fact that I didn't yet have the means to effectively pass courses such as English or math, or the ability to successfully learn how to typeI stopped my education for a short period.

But I did not stop writing my poetry. Although there came a time when I began to realize That if I was to continue writing meaningful, insightful poems I needed to learn more. It was at this point that I registered at Northeastern Illinois University.

Being aware that the same restrictions that I had, still applied, I delved into the field of art with the idea in my mind that this would help me create pictures and designs that I could use alongside my poetry. This proved to be extremely productive for me in more ways than I could possibly imagine. My instructors were creative and insightful and I learned many things not only about art but about the possibilities of my own productiveness.

Then because of the mismanagement and improper consultation from the people who were supposedly meant to give me proper directions at Truman College. My veterans' grants ran out. At first I thought this was a disaster but this disaster turned into the best thing that ever happened to me. It allowed me the opportunity to get a computer and the word processing program "Dragon" which was to enable me to achieve greater success.

On the way to achieving this greater success I met some of the finest teachers that I could ever imagine. In fact, the people that I met as I proceeded along this new path were more than I hoped for. They were not only teachers; they were human beings who cared about other people, who went out of their way, to do everything possible, to help their students achieve success.

Not only did I find great teachers, but also guidance counselors who took that extra step, that little bit more time, to understand and help me grow. 99.9% of all the support help professionals I have found since being at Northeastern, are truly wonderful people.

As to my future, it is my plan to write as many books of poetry as I can and also to turn my newfound skill in writing prose to the advantage and enlightenment of the people of the planet Earth. I agree this sound like a big job, a major undertaking. Yet I have been blessed and given knowledge by many people, and this has shown me a new understanding. It is this understanding I wish to show others by any means possible. And hopefully those means will be entertaining along with giving hope to as many people as possible.

IT'S UP TO YOU

From the twelve golden power books

There is no chance, no circumstance no fate
That can circumvent nor hinder nor control
The firm resolves of a determined soul
Gifts count for nothing will alone is great
All things give way before it soon or late
What obstacle can stay the mighty force,
Of a sea seeking river in its course
Or cause the never ending orb of day to wait?
Each well-born soul must win what it deserves
Let the fools talk of luck
The fortunate are they, whose Ernest purpose never swerves
Whose slightest action or inaction serves the one great aim!
Why even death itself stands still,
And waits an hour, sometimes,
For such a will

HOW TO PRAY, TODAY

by Barry H. Mansfield

Dear God that is everything; I love you more each day
Help me, to serve you, in the most effective way
Help me each day to earn my bread
also to forgive, as I would have forgiven, the things I do each day
thy kingdom come thy will be done
I love you more each day

WE

We look ahead and do what we must
through pouring rain and choking dust
are tune we carry through infinities gates
onward ever onward to our fates

IS--IT

By Barry H. Mansfield

I wonder at the wonder in our lives, the, force that
guides us in times of ecstasy and strife
which we feel yet never see, like wind moving
against our naked face or the smooth
invigoration of slippery water, flowing along our flesh.
Those forces within us that drive us to wonder, or to panic
as the story of our existence unfolds before us
and within us, which says, push forward
against all that stands within our way
I ask what this thing, which presses upon our beings,
Is it from within or without, this
Uncontrolled or controlled emotion that directs the outcome of our existence
is this that, which we all revere?
I asked
Is—It

TIME IS PRECIOUS

by Barry H. Mansfield

Between the long minutes and short years
our, the memories of our lives
exquisite seconds, anxious hours
blend into a funnel storm of existence
swept through the world, at a tremendous pace
in the center of this storm of life, there is peace and tranquility
yet if we move towards the edges of this maelstrom
our perceptions, shift, and we may be blinded by the swirling storm
of amazing sights, sounds and emotions.
The longer we exist within this swirling, twirling, dazzling spectacle
more precious the minutes of wonder become,
and the pace of the years sore and plummet like a brilliant Phoenix
on its way through eternity.
Emotion and reason, belief, a desire
it's hard to learn in the time that we have
feeling and emotion, not necessarily the same.

UNIVERSAL MULTIPLICITY

Or something I believe Mite be

by Barry Mansfield

Master, miracle, mystery
Grand design
change of tune, too small to see
multiple vibrations
of infinity
flow through
multiple universes
the woven strands of universal desire
all we know, and all we don't
ever-changing Symphony of realities
light and matter seem to be the same
could this possibly be, end game

CAN LONELINESS MAKE YOU HAPPY?

by Barry H. Mansfield

In reality I can only speak for myself
this is what I have found
I'm not thrilled with loneliness
having people close to you who love you and care
is a beautiful day in a wondrous place, breathing fresh clean-air
drinking clean cool crystal water, truly wonderful!
alas, for whatever reasons, life does not always give us blissful love
therefore, one must make a choice
live in peaceful loneliness
or in a warlike state, which some call love.
BUT WAR is not LOVE
love should be **love**
It should be
a state where people care about the feelings of others
a place where an individual can be what they are
not argue and fight, with hate and strife
a quiet place in which to live a good life.
if you can't have that
THEN Loneliness can bring happiness
it's not perfect,
but I feel it's better than the alternative.

WHAT A THOUGHT

by Barry H Mansfield

I've heard it said, that there is life before death
what a thought
by putting a little effort into this life
it's possible to find happiness
you don't have to wait till your dead
to find happiness
isn't that great, you don't have to wait
there are a few things you might have to learn
like being kind, and thoughtful
definitely trying real hard not to hate
if you really do these few things
which I'm not saying our easy
I think the possibility is really great
that you can make, this life before death
Truly great!
So why wait!
Try to participate!

COMPASSION

By Barry H Mansfield

Compassion is my passion
It's the only way to really be
I must live within my compassion
If I am to be truly free
If I can love all those around me
I can let all them love me
So I'll live within my compassion
And be truly, truly free. So you see
Love, yourself, have compassion
Yes yourself, love yourself, have compassion
It's the only way for you to really be
And you will, Yes, you will, be truly free.

GIFTS

by Barry H Mansfield

Through the miracle of the existence of life
the neurons coursing through my brain are excited
allowing me to perceive the truths of existence
and blessing me with the ability to relate them
to all who wish to hear.
For this I am eternally grateful

LIFE CYCLE

By Barry H. Mansfield

Dependent on nature's flow, are the things we call life
one of these things we call man
by whose nature, changes occur
and is not man part of nature, by whose very nature changes occur.
Earth, Sun, and rain start the processes, as we all should know
from this Trinity, the grasses grow
each element within its place. This miracle happens in time and space
awareness is the key, it should also be our destiny
we should try to keep in mind, as we build our megacities
that we are only bit players in this ongoing play
that are actions affect not only today
but the total sum of this planet's life
for all Its History.

YESTERDAYS GOWN

Yesterdays gone it was only a dream
Of the past there is only remembrance
Tomorrows a vision thrown on hopes screen
A will-o-the-wisp a mere semblance
Why morn & grieve over yesterdays ills
Or paint memories pictures with sorrows
Why worry or fret for worrying kills
Over things that won't happen tomorrow
Yesterday gone it shall never return
Peace to its ashes and calm
Tomorrow no human has ever discerned
Still hope trust and faith are its balm
This moment is all that I have of my own
To use well or waste as I may
For I know that my future depends alone
On the things that I do today
This moment my past and my future I form
I can make it want ever I choose
By the deeds & the acts I now perform
By the words and the thoughts that I use
So I fear not the future or morn for the past
Cause I do all I'm able today
Living each moment as through it were My last
Perhaps it is, who knows? Who can say?

A REFLECTION

By Barry H. Mansfield

It's not a pleasant feeling
to want something, you can never have.
your emotions crushed and mangled
simply because your physical form doesn't fit the plan
It's said nothing is impossible
only takes a little longer,
may be true, can't prove it one way or another,
guess, if we lived forever, you could prove or disprove this
…Hypothesis… But we don't!
It really isn't pleasant to, have your emotions stepped on
by a judge-mental, hypocritical world.
Through it's been said, there are million things
you can have,
and a million things you can't.
Even if you understand this,
and try with all your might, to do the best you can
It's really sad, that,
what you want, is not within your space
Still, there are so many things you can have, that, only call for a change of plan.

REALITY

Barry H. Mansfield

THE WAY I Think
Controls my life
It cuts much deeper than a surgeon's knife
Love is so real
You can taste and touch steel
So you know what you feel
YES, life too is real
My heart surely beats
My pulse often quickens
As I run through the nights
Fears sometime beckon
Yet! I keep moving on
For I know what I am
A creature of GOD who is spawned from man
Time never stops
Nor shall it ever return
So I look ahead
And I watch and I yearn
And with love and compassion,
I see myself grow
And though time move on
I KNOW THAT I KNOW!

A HARD PATH

by Barry Mansfield

Karmatic intervention directs my soul, from one generation to the next, I flow. The need to progress, modified by humanities pull, habits that are formed, create your temporal path. Existence, no matter what passions or desires you may chase, might slow you down, still you should know there's more to life than this time or place, and this is part of the flow. You can, if you try, get what you want, keep following your dream. Not even death can stop you. It is a long road, to direct your will, it might take more courage than most beings possess. But you can persevere and pass this test. It's a long hard road, so, direct your will. If you choose to believe that there is no soul, then you must believe that the laws of energy and matter just isn't so. And that Light doesn't make things grow, so live in the moment. Keep your mind on the ultimate prize, realization brings enlightenment, through the twists and turns of unknown times. Our souls have been clothed in many forms, in different times with different norms. Faced volcanoes, wars, and storms, been kings and slaves and all that is between. A shadow of an echo, hard to find, resides within, the unconscious mind.

DYNAMICS OF GENETICS

by Barry H. Mansfield

Multitudes Ebb and flow together in a defined space,
separated by barriers of their own design,
in place, time, and attitude
mixing, mingling, and matching, trying to form true
some maintain their self-imposed solitude
cosmic thought forms of quiet desperation
intangible, unknown, but! Oh! So! Real!
Transcendental senses soak, in the possibility of wondrous experiences
fears, feelings of direction, and desire
freeze the soul like Medusa's gaze
time to plan
the first nanosecond, or before
want to be, set us free
mingling humanity
can we learn, can it be
Is there freedom?
We shall see.

A MIRACLE OF SORTS

by Barry H. Mansfield

A bit of thought, I heard one day, on my search along the way
there is a story of a man, who had a quite extraordinary plan
teach others to care and give, show them how to really live
he was a teacher, said to be wise
believed to have come to expel old and terrible lies
from far and near they came, to hear his plan to stop the fear and pain
at this meeting on a hill, he found, he had an extraordinary amount of mouths to
fill he brought with him a fish and bread and with these things a multitude he fed
it was a miracle of sorts, for many there had brought the same
and
in his name
all did share
HE, got that unrelated group to care
feeding all who were there!

WHAT I KNOW

By Barry H. Mansfield

The sun warms the earth, and makes things grow.
Gravity works,
holds things down makes rivers flow.
The way I think controls my life!
Yesterday's gone, it shall never return.
Change is inevitable
all things must Pass.
Stars will die, so will I
These things,
I know!
Empirical proof does show!
Everything else I've heard or read,
leaves doubt,
forgive me.
I just don't know.
Oh yes, oh yes!
Time is of the essence!

BEING HUMANE SHOULD BE THE GOAL OF HUMANITY

Simple multiplicity

by Barry H Mansfield

I talked of multiplicity on a cosmic scale
now I will try to talk about it in a simpler way
the ability to look at situations from more than one perspective
allows an individual or society to learn and grow
move through life with a strong wind behind their sail
a clean wind not carrying the unpalatable crud
produced by minds that can only see from one direction.
It is necessary for a mind to be free of unwarranted restrictions
progress is made with new approaches, to old problems
so do not expect your children to think the same as you
instead hope that they will learn from what has not worked
then spread their minds in all directions
find the answers that solve old and new questions
through compassionate understanding of all which dwell
among the many realities in which we live.

EXPECTATIONS

Trying to fit an obtuse triangle into a square hole

by Barry H. Mansfield

To be an individual, to think your own thoughts
learn, and grow, make sense of the senselessness
of the world in which we live.
This should be the primary goal of every human being,
fight the ignorance of mass indoctrination
think your own thoughts with careful deliberation
search for knowledge, understand what it is you see
do not let little minds dissuade your creativity
shine bright, let the beam of your creativity flow though,
those without understanding,
It's really useless to hurt them
it's not their fault, ignorance is bliss
they have no idea; of the pain, they cause by this:
A great man once said;
Forgive them
they know not what they do!
(They think, they cause no pain)
To me and to you!
So keep on moving on
TO ETERNITY AND TRUTH

MY FEELINGS

If I and my aspects were different, you would make
a great and wonderful friend, upon our
quest into the future, sometimes we are cut by circumstances
and these wounds can only be healed with the help of A strong,
confident, caring, commitment, those who display these attributes are
the ones who make life worth living. I perceive you as such a person,
may happiness and joy find you and comfort you with its warmth.
Once more I say thank you for the opportunity to experience you.

THE FLIGHT

by Barry Mansfield

On fragile wings the monarchs fly

Mexico to Canada, five generations they sore

on gossamer wings they fill the sky, they alone know why

after traveling so far the fifth-generation returns to their home in Mexico

by ones and twos then hundreds then thousands and tens of thousands

they fly to the mountains and follow them to sanctuary
to rest at last among the trees
before their journey
starts again
and
again.

PICKING UP THE PIECES

by Barry Mansfield

Shattered like a broken mirror, the thousand pieces of my life.
Everything I love is being torn away from me,
anything that can go wrong, does.
I ask myself, did I do something to deserve this?
When I was young, maybe then, but I've been being good so long
What a self-centered thought that is, like there aren't a million other souls
who haven't been, or are now, in the same place as me.
I know this, still, it's hard not to blame oneself,
don't believe I did anything wrong.
Still I wonder?
It's hard to understand why these frustrating indignities are thrust upon me.
I believe in Karma, but I'm sure this is not the only
possible reason for all things that happened,
Sometimes, life is just life, in all its prismatic,
unintentional, and irrational divergences.
Unfortunately the frustrating misery of my plight remains.
An intellectual understanding of these, to me, horrendous situations
does not quell my plight.
All I have is my will to fight, to try to see my situation as the ludicrous,
though devastatingly, hilarious situations in my life,
keep reaching for tomorrow or just piece, on this day,
look at the situation as some crazy funny play.
Also, it sure couldn't hurt, anything, *to pray!*

SILENCE

by Barry Mansfield

I walk in silence, though the multitudes walk next to me
I'm sure I can be seen, but it seems I am invisible
Is it I, who rejects all I see?
Or is it all that I see who reject me?
I crave companionship, yet it seems to elude me
this has not always been the case.
There've been times of great joy in friendship
I feel I still have much to offer to any who would accept it,
may not be the same things that once were available to me
to give;
yet that which I have now seems so much greater.
Does this matter, if now I cannot connect?
I may never know
still hope is eternal
I know that all things change
I look ahead with optimism
try to see the light that could shine and
illuminating that which abides within me.

MAYBE I DO

By Barry H Mansfield

At this space in time
We only have one world
It's green & blue, full of life
A blessing on us all
Yet we sit alone and wait
Wile we and the world change
Why we're waiting, who knows?
we cry & cry about what is not now,
Then start again
In and on this being where we do dwell
Are all things possible?
Could be, still, don't know
When we were children we wanted to know so much
when grown, we still should

CHAOS: BREAKING POINT

By Barry H Mansfield

Not seeing what's in front of them
They care not--- Money-Power, their only thought,
Grief The only reality!
Violent intensity begins to shimmer in the air!
It isn't fair. It isn't fair. Why does no one care?
Can't they feel the strain that pulls upon the fabric of the lives
we wear! Pressures on societies, burst the seams of reality
What is good for some, causes massive pain for others
They pay no attention to the pain that some endure
Disrespect, just plain nasty, who do they think they are?
Am I not flesh and blood, just as they?
I feel like they don't want me to breathe the same air, they do!
Pressure, pressure, how much can I bear?
"God" help me, this isn't right, give me a break
All I know is I'm hurting, bad, I'm mad. I'm so mad!
I don't know what to do, where to go, who to talk to,
Talk! Who the hell wants to talk! I want to do something
something bad, real, real bad.
Don't know which way to turn, or what to think.
I want this to stop, but it doesn't, stop, just gets worse,
my mind begins to unravel like a shattered piece of twine
I fall into a ravine of hate a hundred meters wide,
I melt with volcanic rage
as I melt, I flow into the streets, no longer a thinking Being,
But a primal thing, caring not, moving to a savage beat,
hating everyone and everything I meet!
My head is filled with liquid fire,

Striking out at anything, rampaging, the flames grow higher,
what's this mad desire, destroy, teardown,
The flames burn higher, greed, lust, just like them
I feed the greed and desire, I am the fire.
I just don't care, I want my own, take it now,
make them bleed their liquid fire.
I see lights, here noise, means nothing, must feed desire!
Burn, burn, burn, teardown, take, I want mine, Now, Now, Now, I will get mine!
Rampaging through the streets, for hours without end
(Energy expended.) I begin to feel once again, my mind
starts to real, as my senses I barely feel, numbness, recedes,
I look around, **oh God!** What have I done!
There is no pleasure, there is no fun,
This was good for no one.
Mangled, wreckage, people torn and bruised
I'm so tired, want to hide, all around me disaster.
The person I am begins to feel, what I've done is more than real.
Sadness, shame is what I feel.
I pray to **God** for a better deal,
something kind, loving, and real.
It is my hope that one day all will know
that all mankind does feel,
then learn to live and love it together.

KINDNESS REMAINS

By Barry Mansfield

Beyond our time, acts of kindness remain

through joys, wonders, sufferings and pain

kindness flows, goodness is maintained

the opposite is also true
SO
try to love and care today

give the world a chance
SO
tomorrow could be a better day
in a truly wonderful way,
it is for peace I pray

L=HP∞

By Barry H Mansfield

Life = humanity's potential to the power of infinity.
Macro, Mezzo and Micro

BELIEVE IT OR NOT

by Barry H Mansfield

It may be
that
our bases maybe from different places
but all things being equal, were all part of the human race
and the trials and tribulations, joys and wonder
reside and our expressed within us from the same place
And As the leaves on a tree collect the energy of the sun and interact with the
residue of the supernovas of which our earth is made, thereby allowing the tree to
grow producing the seeds of future generations, so does the lives and works of the
individuals of the human race perpetuate the endless possibilities of humanity.

RELATIVITY ON THE MEZZO SCALE

The way an individual sees the world and the position in the world from which they are seeing, causes a relativistic effect in their perceptions of reality. Who you are, what you are, where you are, and the influences of the individuals close to you, in an ever expanding network of social pressures applied upon you by society cause differences in the way reality is perceived.

While it appears that there is a general consensus as to what a particular object looks like, feels like, sounds like, tastes like or smells like. There will be found within the diversity of the human race differences in all these areas, even regarding an item as simple as an Apple. In the case of an Apple the differences will be seen in the verbal description or the artistic drawing or painting or possibly in the way it tastes or smells, and although it is possible for two individuals to perceive this object in relatively the same way it is more likely that they won't.

More important than the perception of an Apple are the perceptions of other human beings with which we share this world, the places where they live and the manners in which they live. This is where our internal interpretations cause the greatest level of relativistic perception. In other words we see what we feel or think is real from the vantage point of the input into our minds caused by whom, when, and where we are receiving these messages. Also the preconditioning that we have received from all those who have touched our lives since the moment we were born until the moment that we perceive.

Another aspect of the uniqueness of our perceptions is the wonder of the synaptic process that directs the course of the neurons as they travel through our brains creating the patterns that we come to recognize as the reality in which we live. The precise synaptic paths that are traveled within our brains are unique to each of us. So it is truly amazing that a generally mutual understanding of the stimuli to which the brain reacts is as similar as it is.

Life tends to diversify but within this diversification is a potential for great understanding. There is a need at least in humanity to formulate a generally understandable way to understand that which is not understood, to make sense of the unexplainable and to rationalize the irrational. In the closer units within the human race we are taught to see possibility in a generally similar manner. Yet as the race diversifies into its many component sections, different belief systems cause perceptual changes in the attitudes and actions of the individuals within these groups. What is seen as rational, proper or real can and is broadly different between the various and in many ways isolated groups of individuals. A simple idea can be made complex simply by the way it is explained within a group. And once the synaptic paths of ideas are carved within our consciousness it is only through acts of self-determination that the relativity of individuals can be aligned to form a greater understanding.

The major benefit in forming a greater understanding is the unending possibilities for new discoveries. Along with new levels of cooperation and compassionate realizations that will be formed, thereby advancing all of humanity in a positive and unending flow into the future.

LOGICAL AND ILLOGICAL REASONING'S FOR BELIEF SYSTEMS

by Barry H Mansfield

Let us talk about reasons for believing anything. There can be many reasons for believing in something. One of these reasons can be that in early childhood everybody around you believed a certain way and being young and still relatively ignorant you take this understanding that was taught to you and make it your own. This is a very common type of reason for believing a certain way about a certain issue.

The second idea on forming a belief system is in two parts, the first being social acceptance. This method of forming a belief system has to do with punishment and reward you were told something, and if you do the thing you were told to do and conform to specific actions as you were instructed to, you are rewarded, and on the other hand if you don't you are punished, or the thought of not believing this view causes psychological pain. And most people not liking to be hurt go along with the ideas expressed, even if there is some resistance, one generally goes along with this belief solely to avoid pain or rejection from other human beings or the personal internal pain caused by one's own fears.

The second half of the second idea is one of observation of other human beings and of the forces that exist within our understanding and/or comprehension. In this system scientific method is sometimes used as a means to an end, but it is not necessary to use true scientific method, but only to find facts that appear to be significant in the formation of the idea. Understanding that in this method the thesis's that are formed even though they may seem quite plausible are still only a thesis. Also in this method one must not allow one's personal psychology and by this, I mean fear of alienation or traumatic circumstance to cloud one's judgment.

REALIZATIONS OF NEGATIVE MOOD CHANGE

by Barry H Mansfield

The first step in the realization and control of negative mood changes is the understanding that all people are human beings and as such we are all capable of and even prone to being controlled or at least strongly influenced by our emotions. The trick as I see it is to form an area within our mind which is solely for the comparison of our emotional reactions. Let us call this area are sensor. In order to develop your sensor you must come to the realization or at least strong belief that the world does not revolve around you that you are not the best or the worst that humanity has to offer.

It is important that you try to see yourself as an integral but separate part of a larger community. And this community has many individuals that are feeling different emotions than yourself, and that although you as an individual might have strong feelings about a particular persons, places or things other individuals within society have different emotional levels about the same particular persons, places or things.

The understanding that all rational ideas are important to the development of a strong and coherent society is one of the main priorities for developing your sensor the acceptance of the idea that you are not the only one who's being influenced by their emotional habits that were developed in early childhood. The understanding of where and when your emotional realities come from is extremely important if you are to redirect synaptic paths within your mind. This redirection or formation of synaptic pathways because they are not readily visible to our senses must be accomplished through the process of visualization.

There are many paths or processes which will lead you as an individual to this very personal ability of redirecting or creating new synaptic pathways. Let me say at this time that this ability is not something that comes simply because you want it to, the processes which allow you this ability take hard work and many hours of concentration. Some will find the process extremely difficult while others will be able to grasp and Institute what they find in a relatively short period. But whether long or short all human beings are capable of developing the understandings which are necessary for this process.

IT'S UP TO YOU

From the twelve golden power books

There is no chance, no circumstance no fate
That can circumvent nor hinder nor control
The firm resolves of a determined soul
Gifts count for nothing will alone is great
All things give way before it soon or late
What obstacle can stay the mighty force,
Of a sea seeking river in its course
Or cause the never ending orb of day to wait?
Each well-born soul must win what it deserves
Let the fools talk of luck
The fortunate are they, whose Ernest purpose never swerves
Whose slightest action or inaction serves the one great aim!
Why even death itself stands still,
And waits an hour, sometimes,
For such a will

LOOKING BACK

by Barry H Mansfield

I watch the ancient evil in the faces of today
it hasn't changed, still the same
an ugly game a real shame
it preys on love and beauty
anything that's good
its real goal, is that good and bad should be misunderstood
it strives to cover the world in the darkness
of misery and pain
don't understand the real purpose or what it has to gain
what I know that must be said
truth and love are good
so, teach this to your children, and hope you're understood

FREEDOM

By Barry H Mansfield

I've never met standardize child
most I've seen are spicy a little wild
human beings who need to grow
learn to know which way to go
within and through this awesome flow.
Not stamped or molded with an iron fist
a wellborn soul fluid and open to its choices
the many paths down which they could go
reality for reality's sake
give them social justice
don't trap them in the prison of old false mistakes
love and compassion let them be what they can be
the choice is ours
I say make them free

OUR FUTURE

by Barry H Mansfield

As we travel among the stars, on our hot rock of blue and green
peering into the universe, with crystal prisms and waves of force
Hoping ever hoping to see, what can be seen, in the largest of all scenes
looking for the answer, are we alone, have we been seen
are there others out there, will they except you and me
some ask with fear and dread, others with enlightening hope
regardless this is humanities new frontier
going back in time with the speed of light
looking for new frontiers within our site
fighting unnecessary fears
these could be our golden years
space- time our path into the future
as we travel among the stars, on our hot rock of blue and green

FUTURE

by Barry H Mansfield

Moving on into the future through the power of the mind
turning thoughts into reality, the world in which we live to be defined
evolution or Digression, ridiculousness or the sublime
new generations of humanity will dwell in and refine
good or bad, right or wrong these things change as time goes on
ever-changing, rearranging adjusting to their times
what was bad becomes good what was good becomes mundane,
because of the pressures of an age.
All these things will happen like the turning of a page
it is we the elders of this day, who must try to guide times movement,
in the most effective way

FOR RANDALL SCOTT MANSFIELD

My Brother
If it's true, know what to do
Do you?

by Barry H Mansfield;

Try to be a righteous soul
though fantasy does take its toll
read and talk and dwell on it
conservation of energy, seems, to make it fit
don't believe in heaven and hell
what will happen, who can tell
there are books, written long ago
by those who also wanted to know
they thought, there is a steady flow
So
Men could learn and really grow.
They believed
each could make their own
done right
a wondrous future would be sewn
Blossom into truth and peace
finally
understanding what is shown
that which *is,* could be known.

PROGRESS

By Barry Mansfield

Innovation that's key!
Finding ways for you to be
look for what you must know
engage your energies into this, and sow!

... Sand falls...

... Time flows...

Eventually, all is buried!

So that like a Phoenix that is reborn
the spark of an idea
can show you how to open the door.

If It is to be. It's up to me

it may not last

but for a time

the spark of idea will be set free

and become part of eternity.

IN·TER·SECTION·AL·I·TY

ˌin(t)ərsekSHəˈnalədē

Barry H Mansfield

Intersectionality makes me like you and you like me

except were different can't you see

I'm down on you, you're down on me

guilty of the same atrocity

does it really exist, in reality

to me it's you, to you it's me

cause if it's you, then I can't be

guilty of that atrocity

when I see you, you're not me

this is true but what's the reality

were all human can't you see

the way we look at each other

forming this prejudice opinion

as to what it is we see

in relations between you and me

that's the only atrocity

I can see

I AM

by Barry H Mansfield

I am, what I am
but I wasn't always this way
I used to be something else
or more accurately, someone else
that is to say, many, someone else's
who they were, what they were doesn't matter much right now
yet there they are, still behind me, with something still to say, in their way
some were greedy, some were wise, some had the spark of madness in their eyes
they were me I was them, that was then, this is now
now I'm me, that's plain to see still wanting to be allowed to be
To be what or whom you say?
Everything, that I can be!
Though the weight of them lies heavy on the matters of today
I'm not them anymore
because you see
IN this moment
all I can be right now is
me.

FUTILITY

Crazy fight black-and-white, skin is skin there is no sin
when will we learn, there is only one world
fish swimming in a sea that's you and me
fish are fish can't you see
many differences there can be
each thinks it's living in its own reality
because of this no great societies will ever remain
also, our future we may not sustain
if we are to win eternity
we must be like leaves on a single tree
which grow, and fall, and grow again
this is the way; we take our part in destinies-infinity!

HOPEFULLY IN THE FUTURE

by Barry H Mansfield

Whether you hear me, now, or not
hopefully the words I write will one day become known
I write not for glory, or money
but with the need to advance the human race.
Though my poems might seem simple
they are a statement of reality yet to come
a vision that, I, see, and wish to pass on to the future
the wonders, that are, and wonders, that could be
that move through time and set us free
a gift for all who will ever be, to open their eyes to a timeless reality

HUMANISTIC APPROACH

By Barry H Mansfield

Inspired by Philosophers, Charles Mills and Mark Rockwell

Intersectionality the many-sided key
shaped by oppression and privilege
must somehow fit the lock, that will! Set mankind free!
Personal Response Association, a thought to forge the key
An understanding of the hierarchy of privilege and oppression
a mighty task, a humongous deed,
there is no way around it. There's nothing else to do.
A dealing with reality, that must be addressed,
a change in understanding, a readjustment of the self,
throughout all society, to the very depths of our being.
A true comprehension, and justice as never known before,
waits with celestial understanding, behind this massive door.
This lock, this door, and key,
will be formed from every discipline
within humanity.

TO REACH THE STARS

By Barry H. Mansfield

With just two things, we can reach the stars
gravity control, and matter energy manipulation
we're well on our way, we started yesterday
from wind and water, to magnetism and atomic understanding
we've come a long way
it took us a long time to get started
but once we did
the progress of our understanding is increased X potentially
in the scheme of things, we started only yesterday
like the penny doubled every day
our knowledge grows
in every way

NOVA

by Barry H Mansfield

The sky fell, nobody died but neither do they live
dematerialized, sucked into a giant buffer
each soul, digitalized, miniaturized
neither conscious, or unconscious merely the potential to be.
The question is, is there a miracle to set them free
there was a danger, to our sun, you see
10 billion in number were we
we had time, we had a choice
1 million ships or one, to set us free
what was to be our reality
as you can guess we chose the latter
a giant ship a mile in circumference, 10 stories high
a crew of 1000 to live or die as the centuries past by
our races hope, in time and space
a hope to find a special place, where we could reconstruct our race
so out we went out in space and time
to seek a miracle sublime
a world blue and green
a place of life and growth, beautiful sun shine

FORGOTTEN DREAMS IN TIMES ABYSS

by Barry Mansfield

The road is long, with many twists and turns upon the way
hopefully you learn and grow, gain wisdom, become better every day.
So many thoughts, so many plans, youth's energy comes into play,
your mind like light through a prism shine's
redirect this light, turn it back to clear true light
focus
a single light try not to let it dim, no matter, no matter how dim
be not attracted to a lovely whim
keep your eye on the one true star, follow it no matter how far
be not disturbed, by pleasures or by pains, ignore the mighty torrential rains
remember, what started you on your path
through the trials and tribulations
remember,
your dreams in times abyss

THINGS COME IN WAVES

By Barry Mansfield

Inspiration Desperation
Manic pleasure----manic pain
Brilliant sun shine, torrent rain
Nothing simple, quite insane
Memories, vehicle of hope
Hope, relieves the strain
we can remember and learn
be whom that we want to be
Without struggle we are doomed to self-indulgence
It's not simple; still it's worth the time
Time, of which there is so little
Within which, we have so much to gain
Remember the past, Look to the future
Live the minute, this is the way; to a better day

WE REALLY DON'T

by Barry Mansfield

We really don't have to, it's really not necessary
to destroy the only world, we have
I realize, that greed and the need to pretend you're better than everybody else
runs rampant in our society's
I understand the need some people have to keep everybody else ignorant
So, they are easily taken advantage of
I even see, how large segments of the population of Earth willingly go along
with these horrendous acts
I realize it's hard to educate people who really don't want to be educated
unfortunately for us to survive
I see that self-realization through education is not a luxury it is a must
if our billions are not to be destroyed
our world to stay green and blue and not turned into a ball of dust
we need a new idea
money and an artificial economy based on greed is not what we need
we need an economy based on people with justice and trust
the alternative could be a dead pile of dust

UNDERSTAND

by Barry H. Mansfield

The proliferation of education must be started at once
it is necessary for our sphere
that we eliminate or at least slow down, the hate and fear
and the perpetuation of the destruction that it does incur
as I said before, compassion must be our passion, it is the only way to be
so that we can use are creativity, productively
I believe in mankind's endless possibilities
yet I still see its endless atrocities.
What can be done?
The question should be asked what is true education?
What is our reality?
How can we best move through it with dignity?
How can we find a place within it?
And move forward through our time
to a future which is both yours and mine
in the path laid out by what we call divine
personal and communal creativity can turn the key
that opens the door, to opportunities
that rid our world of unforgiving animosities

BEFORE TIME

by Barry H Mansfield

Before time, there was a space
And in this space, there was a face
That gazed upon its face
And saw eternity in its eyes.
Alone! Just It!
This would not do!
But it knew, it knew! Just what to do!
And how and when and where it should.
It started time within its space;
And with love and grace,
It fills this space
At an ever, ever expanding pace!
It knows
It grows
It is I Am; I Am It is

COMPASSION

A correction from Thrown out of the Garden

by Barry H Mansfield

Compassion is my passion
it's the only way for you to really be
you must live within your compassion
if you are be truly free
if you love all those around you
you can let all them love you
so, you see
love yourself, have compassion
it's the only way for you to really be
yes, yourself
love yourself have compassion
and you will, yes, you will be truly free

NEED AND DESIRE

By Barry H Mansfield

I need a love that comes on soft fluttering wings
That Grows into a torrent of passion.
A rainbow of desires
A soft warm fuzzy thing that leads my soul to ecstasy,
starts as two, becomes as one.
Retaining self through passions flow
Sharing joy and pain without complaint
Knowing no bounds to Its fulfillment,
Moments of tender joy, without end,
a lover, partner, and friend.

SO GRATEFUL

by Barry H Mansfield

I am so grateful,
for all the blessings of my life
I am basically free from all disaster and horrendous strife
I truly need to acknowledge, the goodness that abides with me
sure, there's been troubles, I've been unhappy along my way
but all in all, life gets better every day
little things that happen through time and space are wonder while they stay
so, I decided to write this poem, to say how grateful I am today
May they last as long as I do, as I finish this good life
free from care and worry and especially horrendous strife

FOR A BETTER TOMORROW

by Barry H. Mansfield

A progressive movement in time and space, means
positive advancement for the human race
Only! Looking at the past, emulating outmoded ideas
holds us back from learning that which we could know
so, let us plant our seeds,
to reap the harvest that will grow!
Creative advancement that should be our goal

IN COMMON

Barry H. Mansfield

It's true, we are different, in many ways
Still
we all get hungry! And need a breath of air
and
water is quite essential to our good health
but
we can give thanks, that we all don't think the same
considering
that if we did our lives would sure be boring
essentially
were copied from a master form
though
differences do appear, making us unique
possibly
our need for love, consideration, and respect
can
make us see each other, as we would be seen.

PURPOSE

by Barry H Mansfield

Life is filled with complexity, unlimited ways to look and see
for some it's hard to know, what they should do or be
look for your true purpose
a path you can follow, a destination for your soul
find your reality, a choice that makes you whole
not all can find this place, where understanding quickens
to a vision you can follow, giving purpose to our strife
a goal to give life meaning, a shining beacon to the future
and generations yet unborn
search for this blessing, of knowledge and of will,
find true purpose within your life
be the most effective *human being* that 'you' can be

PUNISHMENT AND PAIN

Loss or gain

By Barry H. Mansfield

It said that Justice is blind, well, sometimes it's deaf and dumb as well!
In the past, gentleman, like, Aristotle, Socrates and Plato
talked extensively about what justice is,
the expounded many concepts, which might seem to be justice
most of these concepts, they decided were not true justice
Unfortunately
over time many societies decided that they would try
the very concepts that these gentlemen and their friends
had already found wanting. Even though these ideas of justice, were unjust,
yes, it is unfortunate that greed and lust for power
mean more than compassionate justice for all.
Now don't get me wrong
there are many wonderful individuals who care deeply for justice
and, the idea that justice is for everyone.
Unfortunately
amassed wealth is power and in all too many cases,
this power of wealth, leads to injustice
so, what am I saying, I'm saying that the inequality of personal power,
leads to abuse, in so many ways for so many people
fortunately
love and compassionate understanding, still exist,
so, there is, still hope, that one day,
we will, find a way.
To not throw justice away

I WEEP

By Barry H Mansfield

I weep for those who know not peace
who plant the foul and rancid seed,
of greed
like all, they search, but never find
goodness of heart, peace of mind
they lust and kill
with all their will
my heart goes out to those they make bleed
yet, which souls will be freed
I think these our the ones who plant the fruitful seed
the seed which grows into the world tree
and blesses all who choose to see
the wondrous future, which might be

OBLIVION OR SOMETHING ELSE

by Barry H Mansfield

Tornadic activity within my mind
looking toward the future I think I'm blind
moving forward losing time
running a race that cannot be won
mire and muck corroded by sin
looking always toward the sky,
still, I want to fly
I ask again, who am I
what to believe, I know so much
for my own sake, must keep in touch
with all the things that I have learned
as I've looked, the worlds turned
hoping for a little more time
trying to repent, a fictitious crime
whirling and twirling as I go
wear or when I do not know?
yesterday's gone was only a dream
the future now, as always
a blank screen
for most of us, quite a scene.

MANY COLORS, EVER-CHANGING

by Barry H Mansfield

Blues and greens, Reds and Brown's golden deserts and tropical ponds
ever-changing islands rise, Bloom. Sink back from where they came
others rise to take their place on our planet's ever-changing face.
Continents flow at a snail's pace, to form new wonders of beauty and grace
a small blue planet as seen from space
we call it home. The human race.

LIFE CYCLE

by Barry H Mansfield

Dependent on nature's flow, are the things we call life
one of these things we call man
by whose nature, changes occur
but is not man part of nature, by whose very nature changes occur.
Earth, Sun, and rain start the processes, as we all should know
from this Trinity, the grasses grow
each element within its place. This miracle happens in time and space
awareness is the key, it should also be our destiny
we should try to keep in mind, as we build our megacities
that we are only bit players in this ongoing play
that are actions affect not only today
but the total sum of this planet's life
for all Its History.

Obsolescence

Obsolescence is the state of being which occurs when an object, service, or practice is no longer wanted even though it may still be in good working order. Obsolescence frequently occurs because a replacement has become available that has, in sum, more advantages than the inconvenience related to repurchasing the replacement.

Reference: http://en.wikipedia.org/wiki/Obsolescence

OBSOLESCENCE

12/3/2014

By Barry Mansfield

Have you ever wondered?
Why it is, that our society progresses at the pace it does
it could be argued, that we are a throwaway society
which creates waste, at an alarming pace
it's not quite as bad as at first glance it may seem
though it must be admitted it is quite extreme
so is the progress of our science in the last hundred years
there is a sad truth about success, although this truth
has existed since the beginning of time.

Throwing away people, is a crime!

Capitalistic, gentrification, modification,
often sad, but part of the plan
on the other hand
with a bit of modification, we may be able to move into the future
without hurting as many people as we do!

A DOLLARS' WORTH OF HOPE

by Barry H Mansfield

There is a phenomenon in this world, which I find quite nice
I call it, a dollars' worth of hope
you can't buy much for dollar, maybe if you're lucky a candy bar
yet, for one dollar you can dream amazing things
peace, freedom, love and personal power could be yours
all things within your grasp, possibility, at least for a couple days
I like putting my hope in a place where I can look at it
a nice little ticket just for me
so, I can dream my impossible dreams
it may not last long, but when this hope fails
for just one dollar,
I can do it all again

PLEASE SEE ME

by Barry H Mansfield

What do you see, when you see me?
Really, what do you think I am, more important, who are you trying to be?
do you have any idea, how you make me feel?
when you Leer at me, and name me a body part,
or something to be used and thrown away!
I'm a whole person, and I like being treated with respect.
I bet you wouldn't like it, if I called you a body part
or thought of you as something disposable
you trying, to be cute, or funny,
Because for me, being mean and small minded
that's a bad way to start a friendship,
or any kind of relationship!
if in some way, you think negativity will get my attention
think again negativity will only make me loath you
or are you as foolish as you sound and look when you approach me in this way
you want me to think less of you? Just keep on acting the fool
are you really trying in this perverted way to get me to notice you?
if so, seeing me as I am, in my entirety, would be a much better way to start.
Understand, I am a person who needs respect and consideration,
not meanness and degradation,
I do understand that your hormones can kick in,
and you become a thoughtless child
or generally disturbed individual
But, I bet, that someplace in you is a real person,
who also wants kindness and respect
so please see me and try to see me in totality.

UNIVERSAL FORMS

by Barry H Mansfield

What is truth? What is justice? What is honor?
What are the forms that are not norms?
They are a universal design,
that exist within humanities soul
they are real, it is possible to understand them
thereby allowing all to becoming a universal whole.
Socrates and Plato were among the first to tell us so,
the question is, how is it that such a man should know?
It was only an idea, a concept, a formulating thought
and here is where the idea of forms does start
within the mind of man with time to think
of things that might be and how they might become

A FLUTTER OR CHAOS THEORY

By Barry H. Mansfield

The butterfly of change
one stroke of its wings, things get strange
ripples in time and space
affect the course, of the human race
a stroke here, a stroke there
vibrations shimmer through the air
fly and flutter on a Summers breeze
brings a monster, to its knees
slow, at first, the wave does grow
it could not guess, it could not know
the tidal surge of this flow
that started from a single beat
of its very fragile wings
a sound so small, still it could bring
the fall of corruptions massive waste,
a single stroke of its wings
Changes things in the cosmic flow of human beings.

ONCE UPON A TIME

by Barry H Mansfield

once maybe I had a snowball's chance
but that was a rather short romance
now all that's left is a frustrating reality
of a squandered prosperity
that really never seen actuality
still dreams are dreams
and the impossible is no less improbable
the same hope that moved me forward then
still resonates through the eternities of my soul
and my visions still quest through time and space
so maybe that snowball hasn't melted yet
Hope is eternal
Anyway, is there something better you have to do

HOW SHOULD I KNOW

by Barry H Mansfield

Before I knew, what happened or how it came to be
there was a disruption in some of the patterns of my mind
which set me on a path chaotic and ill-defined
although it's been filled with wonder
adventure and romance
it is a lonely frightening road leading forward never back
many things encountered; many gained, many lost
caught in the quagmire of existence, yearning to be free
looking for help, inside, or outside of me
nothing I find seem strong enough to tear me from the muck
the defects of my humanity, fight hard against my will
and yes, at times it's quite a thrill
followed by moments of misery and pain
but even in these times, there's usually something to gain
still, to lift myself above it, this, really is my goal
or at least stay on top of it
and I believe this takes another, who can remind me
in a way I can accept and understand
and help me out of my quagmire
and travel on dry land

IMPECCABLE

by Barry H Mansfield

I am of being of impeccable mind
my understanding is, life sometimes is not what it seems
I look to the future with hope and goodwill
yet sometimes what I perceive
is a vision of things that causes a debilitating chill
it's not my nature to worry and fret
I do not believe that the future is already set
and with my will alone my destiny I form
what now is strange, may one day be the norm
believing in my body, soul, and mind
and of the ever-changing possibilities in space-time
leaves me free to search my being
for what can be found
by using the power of impeccable mind.

I'M FINALLY A BELIEVER

by Barry H Mansfield

It happened just the other day and now I to believe
that all I thought that I know, is not true, we are deceived
it had to do with population growth
it was getting out of hand, then like magic
it fell in line, at first, I could not understand
I thought about all I see, all I've heard
this is what I find, in the wanderings of my mind
I don't expect you to believe a single word of what I'm about to say
but I don't care, because it doesn't matter anyway
it's true, that within certain parameters we are free to live our lives
the illusion of freedom makes us much easier to control
in fact, it makes us willing to perform our assigned role
our world is pushed in directions that suits someone's will
I don't know why, or what, that purpose is, or if it's alien or homegrown
but it is a force which has control, and steals our free will in major things
such as peace and war and who will live or die, and when and why
it controls our health and welfare
the direction that our future takes
not only as individuals, but as the human race

BEGINNINGS

by Barry H Mansfield

Shadows dissipate into a golden light
fears evaporate from site
hope and trust form the dwelling in which to live
compassion's love these things to give.
The way through eternity now is crystal clear
advancement of knowledge, wisdom, and right
trust, understanding the spreading of truth's light
will keep you free
while causing the furthering
of humanity.

WEALTH AND FREEDOM

by Barry H Mansfield

Education and information a new source of wealth for our nation
Zero- point energy will set us free, supplying
enough energy for the rest of eternity
electro-magnetic gravitas revolutionizing transportation
giving us freedom on our planet and access to the stars
what I wonder this will be
but first we must escape the grimy hands of the energy industry
unfortunately, the military industrial complex controls everything we see
gaining freedom from the greedy creeps, won't be easy
a major push for educational superiority is the key
the development of the minds and souls of our children is a must
let our world be known for the knowledge and wisdom we possess
this should be our goal to attain control
of who, what and how we are to be
make heaven are planet's destiny
with unlimited love and spiritualty

GUIDANCE

by Barry H Mansfield

Be there a benevolent being somewhere in time and space, who would help;
guide this seeker in learning to control their destiny?
I asked humbly and with respect
For their counsel
I am tired of keeping only my own
I need a trusted friend, an advisor
compassionate and wise
to help me sort the truth, from the lies,
a being whose ego does not rule their existence
whose existence is ruled by compassion and love
if there be any who are so inclined
I would give to them
my love and gratitude
to the end of time

EMBRACING

by Barry H Mansfield

The many arms of compassion, understanding, and love
reaching to the souls caught in the illusion of despair
a force trying to alleviate human despondency
with gentle respect for unproductive free will
those who know must try to show
that hope is there for all to see
that reality can be changed and rearranged
through kindness, respect, and ultimate acceptance
of the hidden reality
that all our part of the one
and it would be most beneficial to remember
as the old saying goes
"do onto others as you would have them do unto you"
because we are all part of the whole
and
love, understanding and compassion
blesses not only others but also yourself.

GOOD NEWS

by Barry H Mansfield

It's going to happen, of this I'm sure
the fourth turning is almost here
so be joyful and of good cheer
be secure and lose your fear
peace and love are very near
enlightenment of body and of mind
the human race is about to find
together, yet, separate we shall stand
as we form the brotherhood of man
knowledge and understanding you will see
is more than possible,
it will be.

CHILDREN OF THE FUTURE

by Barry H Mansfield

Children of the future, come, and sing your song of peace
let the melodies of life renewed
be clearly heard, so hate and greed at last will cease
souls that know compassion song, bring prosperity and truth
I welcome with open arms, the wisdom that you bring
refresh the earth, make songbirds sing
the sweet refrain of life renewed, the chance to start again
remembering a wisdom long forgot, bringing a blessing to humanity
through wisdom, lost or hidden for what seems an eternity
but now at last the time has come, for those of grace and beauty to abound
their numbers as they increase to populate with the spirit of belief
dispel archaic ignorance with grace and compassion's love
I welcome you with open arms, as you appear my joy does increase
I see you come, I hear your song of peace

REBIRTH

by Barry H Mansfield

Born on to this world, a man of wisdom, wealth, and fame
Adam Ezekiel Moses his name
a mind of crystal clarity, a shining light for humanity
born on winters solstice day
from the moment of his arrival, the world is not the same
the warmth and beauty of his soul
encouraged, love and wisdom to increase each day
his very presence brought understanding
eased suffering and pain
Born into the world, the world is not be the same
goodness and understanding increased at lightning speed
his humanity unbounded in the aspects of his being
the contours of his visage bold and shining bright
a symbol for humanity to end its long dark night
a new vision for the world
a path to set things right
Born into the world a man of vision and sight.

REMEMBERING

by Barry H Mansfield

What must I do to let my intellect flow?
allowing the articulate expression of that which I know
it's clearly saved, all that I have learned
knowledge and understanding
Long studied hard earned
I see so clearly when I looked inside
When I try to bring it out all it does is hide
sure, glimmering's and pieces these I can touch
but, the fullness of understanding not so much
yet even as I say these words, I know they don't apply, all of the time
I've been there when my mind was clear and flowed like a fast-paced River
unjammed by logs, or rocks, or dams
free and clear to express all the wonder that I know
yet, unfortunately at times there's something there that inhibits this flow
and it is embarrassing and sad, this lack of access that occurs
even though I still do grow
I really, really, would like to know
How I can free the currents of my mind.

THE TRUTH OF LOVE

by Barry H Mansfield

Love is a multi-faceted phantasm
a specter of light, sound, touch and, spirit
it exists freely for all those who are willing to accept it
bestowed without conditions or demands
it is a force of nature, it understands.
Still, sometimes there's confusion about what it really means
and though it is professed, it is not always as it seems
some use it as a weapon to make demands on other's souls
in truth it's not demanding, and makes no impossible requests
the truth is unconditional its freedom and its light
that dissipates our fears and allows us to know peace and joy and
learn and grow without the decay of hatreds unrelenting press.
So, give and take it without fear, never be alone
and no, it never shames or blames, for that is not love,
what it is, is comfort and support
that allows us to be free, and gives us leave to be the best that we can be

VIBRATIONS

by Barry H Mansfield

Betwixt and between things seen and unseen,
are the vibratory energy is of eternity,
energy, space-time, and momentum are the building blocks of reality,
defined by the relative position and perceptions
of the vibratory rate of our lives
matter and energy are all vibratory experiences,
call them the music of our lives
and like all music it is the musician who manipulates
or controls the tempo, beat and timing
of their own creation.
Our thoughts are vibrational energy, we have
the ability to control the songs of
our life, altar energy, space-time, and our perceptions,
we can understand reality and its
basic structure by understanding the rhythms and
the flow of these vibrations, everything we
experience in life is a matter of vibration, so, yes are
thoughts are vibrational energy and affect
things in are lives, hate is a vibratory discord
on the other hand love is a melody
what will the sound of your life be, will it be discord or melody
you can create your own reality
you can be happy, healthy, wise and free
truly control your own destiny

SOME PEOPLE

by Barry H Mansfield

Some people, won't let other people be
they attacked them because of their own insecurity
the way I see it
if you don't have something good to say, don't say it
even if you see a problem if you can't explain it in a nice way,
don't
by that, I mean non-judgmental and productive
skip the meanness and the holier than thou
friendship, is a form of love, which should not be mean and nasty
it should come from the soul's boundless peace
some people think that being harsh and sarcastic is a form of love
my sympathy and hope I give
to see them find the truth
escape the self-perpetuated misery that meanness brings
find the fulfilling contentment of compassion's love
give more than they receive
know the blessings that peace and kindness bring.

MEMORIES

by Barry H Mansfield

The fleeting moments of our times, how intense they are
as they reveal the memorable interactions of our lives
pleasure and pain both there to gain, alas never again
to be
for they are gone with only memory to sustain
each moment rare and precious, some sour others sweet
they were there, now they are gone.
So, filled with people, and with things
I rushed from one into the other thinking they would never end
and without judgment for good or bad, I replay them in my mind
the changes that these moments brought, I never could have guessed
at the happiness and pain that I was to gain or repress
the wisdom and the weight
my mind Soares even as my body is pressed by gravities pull.
I wonder if these same things are repeated in each segment of eternity's flow
there to feel the joy and pain to live and love, new memories there to gain
feeling the ecstasy and the agony of life's tenuous flow
all the treasured moments, gone, never more to be
there, only, as memories that took place in space and time
the remnants of what has been
truly, this is all that is mine.

I'M FINALLY A BELIEVER

by Barry H Mansfield

It happened just the other day and now I to believe
that all I thought that I know, is not true, we are deceived
it had to do with population growth
it was getting out of hand, then like magic
it fell in line, at first, I could not understand
I thought about all I see, all I've heard
this is what I find, in the wanderings of my mind
I don't expect you to believe a single word of what I'm about to say
but I don't care, because it doesn't matter anyway
it's true, that within certain parameters we are free to live our lives
the illusion of freedom makes us much easier to control
in fact, it makes us willing to perform our assigned role
our world is pushed in directions that suits someone's will
I don't know why, or what, that purpose is, or if it's alien or homegrown
but it is a force which has control, and steals our free will in major things
such as peace and war and who will live or die, and when and why
it controls our health and welfare
the direction that our future takes
not only as individuals, but as the human race

EVER ONWARD

by Barry H Mansfield

In the beginning, was the source of creation
unbounded potential
although it can manipulate itself, this, creative force was only one thing
it had the will and desire to create
so, it did
it expanded itself into the universe
time and space became reality
its spores of potential sang the songs of creation
light merged onto the darkness
matter and energy appeared to be
the galaxies took shape
within these each star created planets
the potential of intelligent life was everywhere
the spores of creation became individual intelligence
each adding to the creative knowledge of the source
it is the future, it is the past
we are part of its creation
moving
ever onward in its creation.

Printed in the United States
by Baker & Taylor Publisher Services